The Clouds of War
The Speeches, Travels, and Comments of

John B. Moullette, Ed.D.

During the Cold War

DEDICATION

This journal is dedicated to my Mom and Dad — Margaret Philipsen and Clarence Earle Moullette — who, by example, taught me to be aware, to be involved, to be articulate and to be responsible. They truly were sages.

CONTENTS

ACKNOWLEDGMENTS

My thanks to Leland Dirks, who encouraged me to collect these writings in a single volume and to publish them.

1 BEFORE PRESENT

From August 1912 through August 1925, elements of the U.S. Navy and American Marines were engaged in military actions in Central America in what became known as the Banana Wars. The actions taken were in defense and protection of nations, people, and property. The involvement continued throughout World War I in Europe and beyond.

When those sailors on their destroyers dropped anchors off the coast of Nicaragua and those Marines who took to the landing nets at the command of "land the landing party," they would not have known nor could they have imagined they were taking "the point" for a century of war.

2 INTRODUCTION

The Cold War did not just burst onto the world stage as a result and the consequences of World War II. It crept up over eight decades and – at least – two generations in the 20th Century of political, cultural, religious, and economic changes. In that time, the peoples' of the world experienced two national revolutions, two world wars, and an economic depression that had international consequences and brought about world-wide changes in class attitudes – broadly – about freedom and citizen representation in affairs around them and that had an impact on their lives at home and abroad.

This is not a treatise on the causes and results – or the impact – of those changes. It is an account about the involvement of one individual who participated in those events over the decades, especially during the Cold War, and who felt it appropriate to share his experiences and to express his opinion as human beings should have the right and obligation to do without recourse.

3 THE STORMS BREW

Events and Actions Leading up to the Cold War
1914 to 1950 and Beyond

World War One – 28 July 1914 - 11 November 1918

A calamitous war between the Central Powers of Europe and the Allied Powers, which eventually drew the United States of America into the conflict on 06 April 1917

Treaty of Versailles – 28 June 1919

The events and causes of this four year plus world tragedy are best outlined by Pulitzer Prize winner Barbara W. Tuchman in the book *The Guns of August*.

Two of the best and defining, anti-war novels emanating from the Great War are:

- *All Quiet on the Western Front* by the German Great War author Erich Maria Remarque – published 29 January 1929
- *Paths of Glory* by British writer Jeffrey Archer – published 03 March 2009

Japanese Invasion of Manchuria – 19 September 1931

Spanish Civil War – 17 July 1936 to 01 April 1939

Japanese Invasion of China – 07 July 1937

Aerial bombing and sinking – in the Yangtze River, China – by Japanese forces on the USS Panay – 12 December 1937

Nazi-Soviet Non Aggression Pact – 23 August 1939

German Invasion of Poland – 01 September 1939

Declaration of War on Germany by Britain and France – 03 September 1939

Germany launches Operation Barbarossa on the Soviet Union – 22 June 1941

Japanese naval forces attack the American naval forces at Pearl Harbor in the Territory of Hawaii – 07 December 1941

America declares war on Imperial Japan – 08 December 1941

After a Declaration of War by Nazi Germany and Fascist Italy on the USA, America declares war on both – 11 December 1941

Italy surrenders to the Allied Powers – 08 September 1943

Germany surrenders – 07 May 1945

Japan surrenders – 02 September 1945

Chinese People's Republic (CPR) formally established – 01 October 1949

North Korea invades South Korea – 25 June 1950

The Korean War begins with Communist China and the Soviet Union in support of the North Koreans, but challenged by the United Nations

This unending conflict in Korea is best outlined, understood and reported in the book Brothers At War, published in 2013 by Dr. Sheila Miyoshi Jager, Director of East Asian Studies at Oberlin College, Ohio

The Soviet Union Dissolves – 26 December 1991

4 BEGINNINGS

Prior to America's entry into World War II, the only international travel or international awareness I had experienced was a trip to Canada and the following of the Third Reich's activities in Western Europe through the local and daily editions of the Camden (New Jersey) *Courier Post* and the Philadelphia (Pennsylvania) *Inquirer* and the *Evening Bulletin*, as well as the Sunday *New York Times*.

The United States, in the fall of 1940 and the spring of 1941, was at peace with itself but was involved in an on-going dialogue as to whether America should or should not go to the assistance of the Allies in Europe against the Axis Powers – Germany and Italy. The latter two (2) nations were fascist and diametrically opposed to the two (2) major democracies in Europe – Great Britain and France – and, of course, opposed to the American way of life.

The school year – 1940 to 1941 – was a bad year for me. I was in the Eighth Grade at Burrough Junior High School in Camden and I was doing poorly. Of a possible 105 points to attain an "A," I was only able to muster 42. I had straight failures (Fs) in English, General Mathematics, and General Foreign Language. Teacher acknowledgements on my report card throughout the year indicated that "I was poorly prepared; I did not try; and I wasted time." The report, also, indicated I didn't turn in my book reports. Interestingly, Geography was not taught that year and History was combined with Citizenship. Looking over that report card in my sixty-seventh year, I can see there was nothing good to be said for me academically during that academic year and – accordingly – I was "retained" in the Eighth Grade for another year.

My "retention" caused havoc in the Moullette family that summer as my father had planned a family trip to his mother's home in Wisconsin and a subsequent trip to Callandar, Ontario, in Canada, to visit the public home of the Dionne Quintuplets. To make the trip as planned, or to stay home and let John attend Summer School to erase the "retention," was the major question at hand. After much debate, the decision was made to "go." This decision was met with my wholehearted endorsement.

We crossed into Canada from Michigan at Sault Sainte Marie and proceeded east to the home of the Dionne Quintuplets, near Sudbury, and then farther on to Toronto and Niagara Falls.

The land across Ontario was not much different from that in Wisconsin and Michigan – timberland, rolling hills and farmland. The people appeared to be the same as Americans except some had "funny" accents, distinctly British with some French being spoken. West of Sudbury, Canadian Indians – probably Menominis or Ojibways – were in evidence but spoke little and gave me to believe they didn't look favorably on the white man who had come to look. I came away with a feeling there was another point of view as far as the settling of the West was concerned.

Toronto looked like Philadelphia and the only difference between the two (2) was that Toronto had more servicemen sightseeing with girls on their arms. Some of the men wore Australian or Smokey the Bear campaign hats, berets, and overseas or barracks caps. The British influence was evident.

Economically, or financially, prices were about the same in the two (2) countries, but when you crossed borders you paid 90 cents American for a Canadian dollar and $1.10 Canadian for an American dollar. That was my first awareness that the value of currency was not the same and that other nations placed a high value on the American dollar.

My outstanding recollections of that trip are obvious, but additionally I did learn that gasoline – called petrol – was more expensive in Canada and was measured by the Imperial Gallon – 20% more than an American gallon. You got more for more or was it more for less? And, it was obvious, Canada was a key member of the British Commonwealth.

Well, America entered the war against the Axis Powers, which now consisted of Japan, on 07 December 1941. For the next two (2) years I would be chomping at the bit to get involved. The opportunity came in November 1943, when I enlisted.

Military service took me – during World War II – to Okinawa, where I learned that on a Japanese-held island there was a distinction among Japanese (warriors), Koreans (laborers), and Okinawans (indigenous). However, they all possessed the same personal traits: honest, hard working, true to their word, and friendly once the fear of death was removed. One had to come away from that experience with the knowledge that not all Asians were alike in their physical characteristics and that all shared a rich culture, however diverse.

North China, too, was in my itinerary and the same personal traits I observed of the three (3) nationalities on Okinawa existed in the Chinese and Japanese on the mainland of China. The Chinese – hard working and honest; the Japanese troops cooperating with the American Marines – loyal and trustworthy. This did not mesh with American wartime propaganda as far as the Japanese were concerned. During the war, we were fed pap about the Japanese that was intended to implore us to show no quarter when fighting the "Jap," which we didn't; but, then, they didn't either. Well the pap served its purpose; but, when the war was over we saw a different and better side of the Japanese than just the samurai.

In China, during the latter days of 1945, I received a letter from my father admonishing me not to return to America with tales of poverty, unsanitary conditions, and graft; but, rather to return with an awareness that the Chinese had a long and worthy history, a rich culture, and a bent for the scientific. I found the Chinese, also, to be industrious, imaginative and capable of hard bargaining.

During my 1945-1946 stay in China, the Chinese – especially in northern China where I was stationed in Tientsen (Tianjing) and Peking (Beijing) – were engaged in a civil war between the Nationalists and the Communists. I don't remember taking sides – other than what American foreign policy commanded, but I do recall vividly that the Chinese Communists promised that when they came into power they would:

1. Abolish prostitution
2. Close down the drug houses
3. Prohibit the use of rickshaws; and
4. Unbind the feet of women.

Considering what I had seen and experienced in China – under the Nationalists – I didn't think the Communist position was all that bad.

Well, I left China with deep and lasting impressions of a vast land, and the Chinese – in search of a different and better way of life.

From December 1946 through August 1949, I traveled to Mexico, the Caribbean islands of Aruba and Curacao with passages between Cuba and Haiti, and to the South American countries of Colombia, Venezuela and Brazil. This travel was done by tank ship for an oil company, which eventually would take me to Europe, the Near East, the Mid East, Malaysia, and the Far East, as well as to Panama. More extensive travels would take place later in my life, but principally in the same areas of the globe.

On a fateful day in June 1950 – Sunday, the 25th – the North Koreans crossed into South Korea and the war of containment began. Most of my friends didn't know where Korea was, but they did understand the implications of the invasion – we were at war again!

I had a vague idea where Korea was located and when I consulted an atlas I found that I hadn't been too far from it on a troopship passage through the Yellow Sea – inbound for Tangu (Dagu) China and outbound for San Diego (Dago). Whatever "we" Americans were doing at that time or whatever we were preparing for in life – all came to a halt for some of us and once gain we found ourselves in the Orient or bound for it. And, of course, the cry went up – "Why?" No easy answers to that question at that time. But, it did cause me to wonder and then to sit down and write my first "international paper" to my dad. The following is the full text of a letter from Camp Pendleton, California – the home of the First Marine Division:

16 January 1951
Tuesday

Dear Dad,

I just finished reading from the *Los Angeles Examiner* the "impeachment resolution" against Dean Acheson which was introduced to the California State Senate by State Senator Jack B. Tenny, Republican, from Los Angeles. I can't help but think that the American people, Democrat and Republican alike, are "fed up" with the Administration and its foreign policy.

The way Truman is appropriating money is outrageous. It is my belief that he is taking anyone's word for it and spending money uselessly and needlessly. At present he is asking Congress for $71.5 billion which would cost each American $468.00.

Don't you think our "foreign policy" is fouled up a bit? What right have we to refuse Red China entry into the United Nations? I think she (Red China) has a right to voice her opinions about what is to take place in the Far East. After all, isn't she a country out there just as Venezuela or Brazil is in our hemisphere? I say, "let Red China into the U.N. and let her voice her vote and her opinions on what is to take place in the Far East."

The needless waste of life in Korea, on both sides, is shameful to the human race. Fighting won't settle anything. The only thing that I can see is being proven in Korea is: "might over what may be right. (Red China being the might.) The problem of Red China vs. the world, or the best part of it, has to be settled at the roundtable and eventually it will be. Red China will be admitted to the U.N. So, the U.N. will have lost the first round. Christ, we did better in the "Boxer Rebellion."

I thought that only Congress could declare war. Why doesn't Congress either declare war against Red China or stop Truman from sending American troops throughout the world? Why should we take the brunt of it all? If the other countries in the U.N. won't supply the needed men and money then we should pull out of Korea and if need be, out of the U.N. and adopt something similar to what Hoover suggests.

The morale of the fighting man is very low. Mainly because the American people aren't behind him. Here at Pendleton most of these men know what war is or what its after-effects are and will be. Just last night at the "slopshute" (beer hall) the men, not one or two but the majority, were complaining about the way we were tricked into this. Everyone seems to have nothing but disfavorable thoughts and remarks about the foreign policy.

These men aren't afraid to fight, it's just that they have no cause to fight. If ordered to, we will, but only because of the obligation we have to each other. I guess it's a form of "brotherly love."

Our only hope is that men our age throughout the world feel the same way and will state so to their leaders. By rebellion or other ways. After the loss of life, and property from the last war everyone should want only peace. I believe that the people of our land want only peace but that the leaders (including Truman) are afraid to admit they are wrong and are ashamed to admit it for fear they will lose face. It looks that way, Dad!

I guess I've tired your eyes now so I'll secure for now. Good luck in your defense job.

Love,
Johnnie

P.S. I may be a rebel but these are my own thoughts and convictions.

Hey, that's not a bad piece of writing for a guy who failed Eighth Grade English, who got a final grade of "C" in English the second time around in the Eighth Grade, a "C" in English in the Ninth Grade, and who "dropped out" of high school in the 10th Grade in October 1943 to enlist in the Marines. If the article shows any sense of symmetry, grammatical correctness, parallelism, noun-verb agreement, and appropriate syntax then applause should be directed to those great English Language teachers at Temple University High School in Philadelphia who tutored many a returning veteran for preparation to enter college. In the fall and winter of 1949 and the spring and summer of 1950, they drilled us in the English Language. And, in 1951 – while in Korea – I was able to graduate "in absentia" with a high school diploma. In 1952 I entered college.

With respect to that piece of prose, let me point out that that letter reached Secretary of State Dean Acheson, hit the front pages of the major American newspapers, was cited by columnist Max Lerner of the *New York*

Post as the most important event of 1951, was referenced in two (2) books: *Master Plan USA* by John Fischer, and *Patterns of Responsibility* by McGeorge Bundy, and caused me all kinds of trouble in the Marine Corps. The Corps doesn't look kindly on those in its ranks who speak out. But, it was not my intention to speak out – the letter was a private letter to my father. The only one in the Marine Corps who seemed to understand was the Commanding General of the First Marine Division who summoned me, looked me over and dismissed me while stating: "Hell, I can't tell you what to write to your father."

The letter, or rather the public exposure of the letter, taught me at least one (1) thing – if you go public with your ideas then be prepared to withstand a blistering response from all quarters. For those who might be interested in the "blistering response," the original letter and countless positive and negative responses to it can be found in the Harry S. Truman Library at Independence, Missouri.

But the letter itself – what was the message?

Well, it was saying at that time:

1. Americans would be content with an isolationist policy. But, we all knew or had learned that couldn't be in a world of quick communications, closer borders and a universal desire for personal liberties.

2. The Executive Branch and the American Congress needed to delineate their responsibilities, which eventually did occur with the introduction of the War Powers Resolution Act of 1973.

3. Red China or the People's Republic of China should be admitted to the United Nations, which it eventually was in 1971.

4. America cannot police the world. It can lead, but it cannot go it alone – a fact that was demonstrated during the Gulf War of 1990-1991, and in Somalia in 1992-1993. *

5. American fighting men always gripe, but when the foray is on and the chips are down they always come through. Nowhere was this better demonstrated than in the American military effort in the Vietnam War.

*And, a fact that seems to be recognized world-wide. At the time of this writing (January 1993) United Nation's (UN) troops are involved in 13 areas of the world – in the north from the Balkans in Europe and in the south to Angola and Mozambique in Africa; and, in the west from El Salvador, and in the east to Cambodia on the Asian Mainland.

Homeward bound from Korea – once again – there was time to reflect on what "Korea" really meant. For the democracies, the "war of containment" was an actuality, since 21 nations fought against the Communists of North Korea and Red China. I personally served with soldiers from Great Britain – England, Scotland, Wales and Northern Ireland; Australia; Belgium; Canada; Ethiopia; and South Korea.

One lasting friendship evolved from that experience and that was with a Scotsman who served with the Royal Northumberland Fusilier Regiment, now deceased.

5 THE INTERLUDE

Two (2) events of portent in international affairs occurred in the world while I was at sea with the Atlantic Refining Company (ARCO) between the years 1946 and 1949: (1) Britain withdrew from Palestine, which resulted in the establishment of the State of Israel, the occupation of the West Bank of the Jordan River by the Hashemite Kingdom of Jordan, and the occupation of the Gaza Strip by Egypt; and, (2) West Berlin was blockaded by the Union of Soviet Socialist Republics (USSR or Russia). Both events would significantly influence the next four (4) to five (5) decades of the 20th Century – the worst century to-date with respect to the loss of life in the world.

And, in June 1950, North Korea invaded South Korea – initiating the American "policy of containment" in foreign affairs. Few Americans were left untouched by that "conflict," which ended temporarily with an armistice in 1953.

For me, the Korean War ended during the second week of September 1951 in the midst of the First Marine Division's Punchbowl Operation. Rotated back to the States and placed on inactive reserve status with the Marines, I returned to sea for a year and entered college in September 1952.

To me, higher education was higher education; so, I entered a small college in southern New Jersey. It wasn't what I expected, but it did give me the opportunity to sharpen my abilities at reading, studying, thinking and writing. However, after two (2) years, I transferred to a second state college in central New Jersey, where – to my delight – students were required to place a greater emphasis on: reflection, accuracy, depth and analysis: the four (4) requirements of an academician at the student, as well as at the professorial levels.

In the meantime, I married and by the time I would graduate in June 1957, I would be raising three (3) children. The requirement of raising a family didn't permit me to delve deeply into my studies; however, I was able to maintain a "C" to "C+" average while carrying 19 semester hours each semester over a two (2)-year period. As an English major, I did take four (4) courses related to international relations and one (1)* in which I was permitted to explore "personal ideas" in any field. Those courses were:

- History 206: Europe 1815 to the Present
- Geography 301: Economic Geography
- Education 404: Mental Hygiene*
- History 404: International Relations
- History 418: Contemporary Problems In Asia

The four (4) professors of those five (5) courses held students to professional rigor and in those courses I managed to maintain a "B." Contrasted with my other grades, the "B" average says something about "demand" on the professors' parts and "interest" on the student's part.

Term papers from those courses do not remain, but I do recall writing – on the basis of at least secondary source research – around the following themes:

1. The "Age of Reason" sparked a desire for both national and individual freedom.

2. The lack of resources – intellectual, physical and material – would divide the "have-nots" from the "haves."

3. Egypt – separated from a monarch – would influence events in the Near and Mid East.

4. International relations, out of necessity and following the course of events in the world, needed to remain fluid and flexible.

5. Asia no longer would be the prostitute of foreign powers, especially of those powers situated in Europe.

Getting through college – financially – during the years 1955-1957 required me to go to sea during the summer months. In this time period, I made two (2) round trips to Banias, Syria, from Philadelphia, and two (2) round trips through the Panama Canal, also, from Philadelphia. In both cases, the lack of economic development was self-evident as soon as one stepped ashore in Syria and as one observed the level of subsistence of those living on the other side of the Panama Canal cyclone fence – east of the Panama Canal.

International events during this period did not remain static. Joseph Stalin died in 1953 – an event which held out some hope that the "iron fist" over Europe would lose its grip. Within two (2) years, the Hungarians would withdraw from the Warsaw Pact (1956) and eastern Europeans would begin voting with their feet, which would result in establishment of the Berlin Wall, and, eventually, the Iron Curtain (1961). The French Indo-China war would conclude with the defeat of the French Forces (mostly German in the French Foreign Legion) at Dienbienphu in 1954. This defeat would bring down France's Fourth Republic in 1958, and at the same time intensive fighting would occur in Algeria (1957) which would conclude with the Independence of Algeria in 1962.

Egypt – under Nassir – would nationalize the Suez Canal in 1956, and this would result in an attack on Egypt by Britain, France and Israel and the occupation of the Sinai Peninsula – east of Suez – by the Israelis, from which the Israelis later would withdraw under pressure from the Eisenhower Administration.

Those were turbulent times in which to attend college and to start raising a family. It became evident in the 1950s that:

1. The interdiction of the State of Israel into the Arab Peninsula between Turkey and Yemen would not be accepted – without a struggle – by the Arabs.
2. The "little brown men" around the world would not continue to tolerate "colonialism."
3. The desire to be free – as individuals – would spur Europeans to take chances at tremendous odds in order to gain individual freedom.

And, to the latter point, Hungarians in the thousands would flee from their homelands and would find their ways to Camp Kilmer (New Brunswick), New Jersey, where I would have the opportunity to witness their plight, while assisting to the attending of their needs as refugees.

In the summer and fall of 1958, I once again would sail – this time around the world – and pass the naval "choke points" at the entrance of the Mediterranean Sea, in the Indian Ocean between the Horn of Africa and the sub-continent of India, the Straits of Malacca between Malaysia and Sumatra, the Taiwan Straits between the two (2) Chinas, and the Korean Straits separating South Korea from Japan.

It proved to be a momentous trip. When it concluded, I prepared a speech for the International Section of the New Jersey Junior Chamber of Commerce (the Jaycees) entitled "Trouble Spots in the World." The full text, presented at a statewide convention of Jaycees, is as follows:

Trouble Spots in the World

America's slow but steady excursion of power throughout the world during the Second World War in pursuit of a successful completion of that war led the United States away from isolationism and into the forefront of world leadership. This was done without a raised eyebrow in civilian and non-governmental circles and without a general awareness that the power structure of the world had changed.

The Truman Doctrine – that policy that guaranteed American protection of Greece and Turkey against Soviet imperialist expansion – was accepted with little understanding by this Nation's citizens that the keystone throughout the world had been laid for the containment of communism. A general air of uneasiness over the military presence of Russia in the Mideast was brushed aside by the public with a general feeling that all would be settled in the world when and if the Russians would withdraw their wartime troops from Iran. This, they eventually did.

This illusion, however, was shattered in 1948 when Russia clamped a total blockade on all land traffic between Berlin and West Germany and accused the Western Powers of violating the Potsdam Agreement – that agreement among the World War II allies that supposedly settled the war in Europe.

Americans awoke on June 24, 1948, to find themselves in another type of war that was to frustrate them for years to come. It was referred to as the Cold War and it was characterized by: blockades, vetoes in the U.N. Security Council, boycotts, walkouts, non-participation, and non-cooperation by the Soviets with their former allies. Those efforts that held some promise of bringing stability to the world were hereafter discouraged. There followed a series of communist aggressive acts that increased world tension. Nationalist China fell to the communists in 1949, North Korea invaded the South in 1950, the French lost their Southeast Asian colonial war in 1954, communist China pressured the Quemoy Islands and threatened Taiwan in 1958, and Lebanon faced and experienced communistic subversion in the same year. The disheartening events went on and on until hardly a spot in the world was not touched and Americans had come to live and accept a chaotic world.

Since the chaos showed no promise of disappearing, a question arose; 'Could future trouble spots in the world be identified and predicted?' The answer appeared to be 'yes' if the causes of trouble could be delineated. The conflicts seemed to resolve around:

• differences in political ideologies

- differences in religious ideologies
- differences in living conditions and economies
- desires for a national identity; and,
- an imbalance of power.

In the main, two political ideologies are afoot in this world: communism and capitalism. The one attempts to make individuals products of the state and the other attempts to make the state a product of individuals. Both ideologies stand eyeball-to-eyeball across three artificial boundaries: the Iron Curtain in Europe, the 38th parallel in Korea, and the 17th parallel in Vietnam. Any attempt – by either side – to dislodge the other from these lines of containment promises a major conflagration.

The continuous prodding of the DMZ in Korea by the North Koreans forces an eternal vigil on our part and threatens the world.

Today, the Mideast is fraught with tension principally because two world religions – Judaism and Mohammedanism – find themselves incompatible in a geographic area that for centuries harbored only one religious thought and where, previously, any attempt to change the status quo in religious thinking was met with violence. The Jews stand as a threat – religiously and economically – to the Moslems; and, the latter is intent on ridding the area of that threat. The former is just as determined to make a way of life as the other is to destroy a way of life.

Two extreme groups are developing in this world: those who *have* and those who *have not*. The latter is getting larger while the 'haves' are pulling away from the 'have nots' at an unprecedented rate. Throughout the world there is poverty; our own country is not excluded. The poor, the depressed, the oppressed are crying out for a greater share of the wealth. And, where their cries go unheeded, the conditions for revolt are outstandingly prevalent! Russia was the first in the 20th Century but Cuba will not be the last to overthrow an inconsiderate and unheeding national regime.

The desire to be strong and independent is a natural, human characteristic. Since nations are governed by humans, the desire of the nations to be independent is simply the extension of the human desire. European colonialism was the first modern institution to fall a victim to this natural desire. In our time, we have watched the dissolution of the British, French, Dutch, and Belgian colonial structures. The dissolution of dependent structures is just beginning. Today, we are witnessing the dismantling of a short-lived quasi-empire brought about by wartime reparations. Okinawa will be returned to the Japanese; but, it will not be, as others have not been, returned without agitation.

Soon, these empires brought about by the need for economic and strategic treaties will be dissolved also, and, also, probably by agitation.

The balance of power is equal today between Russia and the United States. Any attempt to alter the balance on land by either of the two forces threatens to result in a showdown. Eisenhower was aware of this when the Russians moved into Hungary. This lesson did not go unnoticed by the previous Democratic administration when the Russians invaded Czechoslovakia. Any move on our part to thwart that Russian invasion by the use of our troops would have been met with a counter force. Any attempt to offset the balance must be done with increases in land, sea, and air armaments; otherwise, major confrontations will occur.

There, briefly, are the causes of the trouble spots in the world. The causes listed are not all inclusive. The causes, however, are accentuated and extended when powers – even of the same ideology – compete for supremacy. The problems and tensions increase when poverty is coupled with economic and political instability.

The trouble spots in the world will not vanish over night. They will be here for generations. We must learn to live with them if we – as individuals – are to retain emotional and mental stability. But, the causes of trouble must not be ignored!

This nation and the world of nations must face up to the troubles. National and international priorities must be established to save this battered old world. You and I – as we prepare to leave our debts to a new generation – must ask ourselves some searching questions:

- Is it more important to put a man on the moon or to put a man on his feet on this planet?
- Can the resources of the world be raped in favor of the few and to the disadvantage of the many?
- Is it important to promote those political and religious ideologies that touch only a minority of the total world population at the expense of the majority?
- Is it humane to sit by and follow a principle of non-intervention or non-involvement and watch one nation commit suicide, another nation destroy itself in a practice of apartheid?
- Can the principle of free enterprise really succeed in a world marked by so much failure?

The questions like the troubles are not all inclusive. These questions and many more – I submit – will be at the heart of the next generation of trouble spots in the world. Who will attempt to answer them? This Nation, the Soviet Union, the United Nations? Who knows? But, it is certain that this generation of world citizens is only going to hack away at the problems. The next generation of young people and the ones following them will pick up the brunt of the problems in the trouble spots of the world. Shouldn't they be given the opportunity to voice their concerns and express their views?"

That speech followed by a few months the initiation of the worst civil war since the Spanish Civil War of the 1930s and the worst prior to the Civil War in the Balkans in the 1990s. This, of course, was the Lebanese Civil War, which I witnessed from a super tanker (the SS Delaware Sun) off the coast of Beirut as the ship off-loaded Bunker C fuel to the aircraft carrier USS Saipan and as 15,000 American Marines and Army personnel descended on that city, which was to be devastated over the next 30 years.

The turn of the decade saw the Bay of Pigs fiasco, the Cuban Missile Crisis, and the slow start-up of the American presence in Vietnam. The latter episode was to have a major influence on the way I raised my boys and on the way in which many Americans looked at their country as it fumbled and stampeded toward the 21st Century.

6 SPEEDING UP

In the fall of 1960, as John F. Kennedy was beginning his career as president-elect and president of the United States of America, I was beginning mine in the vocational and technical education field of job skills training.

The '60s were to become the most turbulent of years for Americans as we headed into a mismanaged war, the civil rights movement, and a civil war if not a revolution in our cities. Additionally, we were to come face-to-face with our biases and with our morals. And, we would find the two (2) incompatible. In a very real way, during the '60s, we would strive for compatibility in these areas and make significant gains in the human rights movement. But, that was more toward the middle and the end of the 1960s.

In 1961, we experienced the Bay of Pigs fiasco wherein we aborted American support for a rag-tag invasion of Cuba by Cubans for the purpose of freeing Cuba from Castro. Other than placing America in the position of being caught with its hand in the cookie jar, this action did not threaten world peace as long as we were willing to back off and not attempt to imbalance the balance of power between the USA and the USSR. At that time, I thought the endeavor was foolish – sending an ill-trained guerilla force against a Russian-trained and equipped army just didn't make sense.

But, American foreign policy was not my major concern at that tune – "jump-starting" my career was. And, I concentrated on helping to firmly establish a technical institute in southern New Jersey. In the midst of this career endeavor came the Cuban Missile Crisis (1963) wherein the Soviets attempted to install ballistic nuclear missiles in Cuba 90 miles off Key West with the obvious intention of threatening the United States. The threat did not stand as the Kennedy Administration challenged the Soviets with a naval quarantine around Cuba and Khrushchev turned his missile, transporting fleet around and, then, removed existing missiles from the island. For about three (3) days in October we were eyeball-to-eyeball with the Russians and it appeared that life on earth was about to come to an end. There is no doubt the threat was real; but, I found it difficult to believe that human beings in the Kremlin and in the Pentagon would even consider a nuclear war. This episode in world affairs began the crack in American public opinion that would last into the '80s and it was epitomized with two (2) bumper sticker slogans which one chose depending on one's point of view: "Better dead than Red" or "Better Red than dead."

Over in the western Pacific the Americans were supporting – not too enthusiastically – the regime in South Vietnam against a group of insurgents called the Viet Cong (VC). I, personally, did not pay much attention to this since our effort there appeared to be miniscule and centered more on "advising and training" than on overt action against the VC or North Vietnam. But, one day my two (2) oldest boys came home and told me of the Green Beret "down the street" who had just returned home from what used to be called Indo-China. In a short discussion with him, I got the distinct impression that we were in deeper than we were being told or that I was paying attention to.

Shortly, thereafter, a couple of VC "torpedo boats" allegedly attacked one of our navy's ships of the line in the Gulf of Tonkin. To me, this so-called attack seemed to be nothing more than an insignificant incident that could and should have been overlooked. But, the Johnson Administration took it seriously and Congress passed the Gulf of Tonkin Resolution in 1965, which called for the President "...to take all necessary measures to repel any armed attacks...and to prevent further aggression." Open sesame! American troop movements increased to Saigon and the situation began to take on the scenario of another attempt by the Soviets to use surrogate forces to spread communism in another part of Asia. And, that is how I saw it.

The mid-1960s was the apex for all that was perceived to be wrong in America: we were involved in a war that to many made no sense; we were sending the disenfranchised in our country to fight that war; and, we were not providing equal opportunities at home. Our cities and our campuses exploded against it all. Since the war in Vietnam was the focal point of the dissension, I chose to defend our involvement in southeast Asia as necessary in the ongoing battle against the Soviet domination of the world. And, to this point I spoke out in favor of our involvement in that war. This resulted in a broadcast on the Rutgers (University) Report on World Affairs presented during the week of 14 October 1967, and during my employment as a Lecturer in Education at the Graduate School of Education. The full text of that speech follows.

RUTGERS REPORT ON WORLD AFFAIRS
Viet Nam – Committed By Heritage

Eight-tenths of its way through the 1960s, the United States finds itself involved in a dirty little war, thousands of miles from home, on another continent, foreign to its culture, religion, politics, economics, and general way of living. This is a war which few Americans understand; one in which few Americans find interest; and, a war that many Americans find distasteful if not detestable.

Traditionally, the American attitude toward war – any war and especially those involving foreign belligerents – is, it is a poor way to argue differences and it is best that America and Americans not get involved. Yet, here in the second half of the 20th Century, America is and Americans are involved in the Nation's fourth major conflict of this century.

In 1917 and again in 1941, we actively entered two wars on the side of the Allies – two wars which since have been proven to have been initiated by those powers bent on armed aggression and national aggrandizement.

In 1950 and again in 1964, we deliberately and determinedly committed American troops and naked power to thwart the expansion of communism by bullet rather than by ballot. Korea came as a rude awakening to the international responsibilities of world leadership willed upon America and Americans by the rapid disintegration of the United Kingdom -- that power which, for centuries, effectively or ineffectively maintained world order.

Vietnam and American involvement there attests to the harsh facts that the maintenance of world order has definitely passed to the Americans. The struggle there attests also to the fact that either the communists haven't taken America seriously or they feel it is in their best interests to continually test us or keep us actively involved in dirty little wars. They hope that we will become hopelessly divided at home. To the latter – it appears they might be succeeding:

- American statesmen are taking opposing positions not only on the conduct of the war but, also, on whether or not America should even be involved.

- Citizens of the United States are protesting in every conceivable manner against American involvement in the war and the horrible way and business of war.

- Draft-age youth have burned their selective service cards to demonstrate their distaste for the war, and, in several instances

- American servicemen have refused to participate in the course of the war.

On the surface – it does appear that America and the Americans are divided until one takes into consideration that dissent is the right, the responsibility, and the habit of the Americans. The voice of dissent has almost always been raised against government. There is no reason why it shouldn't be so in the case of the Administration's decision to commit itself and its countrymen to the action in Southeast Asia.

Dean Acheson, America's controversial Secretary of State during the Truman Administration's reign over America's commitment in Korea, retorted – when personally criticized for America's involvement in that conflict – that it is good that Americans should question whether the steps the government is taking are right or are wrong. And, he believed it was important that the people have a strong faith in the validity and the reality of the ideals on which this country was founded and on which it endeavors to guide its actions.

Today, as it was during the Korean Conflict and has been during every war that America and Americans have witnessed, it is truly American to abhor:

- The maiming and the killing of human beings, especially the innocent of which many are women and children
- The rising numbers of casualties of which most are the flower and the cream of a generation of young people
- The unnecessary and often wanton destruction of cities and villages, and – ultimately – whole economies; and,
- The unstable conditions in the world that cause us to concentrate a good portion of our wealth and energies on the business of killing and destroying rather than on the imaginative business of living and building.

But, bear in mind: It is not the Americans who have overtly or covertly created the conditions in the world that have led nations to arm, to become suspicious of one another, and to take sides – one against the other.

The Americans have not extended their borders with or without the forces of aggression.

The Americans have not exploited the resources – human or material – of others.

The Americans have not neglected the problems and the conditions of those less fortunate in this world.

The Americans have not refused to support -- publicly and

financially – the peace protecting agency of the world; and, the Americans have not exercised the power of the veto in the Security Council.

However, America has taken the steps necessary to protect its people and its way of life. We may have misunderstood or misinterpreted the intent and the power of international communism as it raised its ugly head at the end of World War II; but, our understanding and acceptance of the realities of an ideologically divided world has changed from one of naïveté to a sophisticated understanding of the opposition. There exists in America today a determined spirit never to be fooled again or to lose our grip in the world of power while promoting and protecting a future order among nations.

We have been conditioned by the events and the times of Iran, Greece, Korea, Hungary, insulting Soviet Russian Premiers, deceit, callous communist officials, fence-straddling allies or former allies, Cuba, and the direction and actions of the so-called People's Republic of China.

On our side of the ledger, we can point with pride to our many governmental and non-governmental contributions to developing nations – contributions which have worked in the cause of peace, not in the cause of war.

Central to American Democracy is America's concern for others and for the rights of man. We believed so firmly in the rights and the equality of man that we waged our War of Independence on the proposition that all men are endowed with certain unalienable rights and that governments derive their just powers from the consent of the governed.

Having won that point, we initiated our form of government on another proposition that it was necessary to establish justice and secure the blessings of liberty for ourselves and for our posterity.

When these propositions were threatened within the framework of our own borders, we set about to ensure that government of the people, by the people, and for the people shall be maintained regardless of the price.

Having entered upon a new role in international living – as a result of America's acceptance of international responsibility during the First World War, America moved to share this new role with others on the basis that as Woodrow Wilson stated it: 'We set this nation up to make men free and we did not confine our conception and purpose to America, and now we will make men free! If we do not do that, all the fame of America would be gone and all her power would be dissipated.'

Wilson wasn't successful in getting America to participate in the League of Nations; but, he did set the stage for a future world order that was to capture the support of America and enlarge its faith in the vitality of our society and the rights of man.

This, then, is our heritage. We have worked hard for freedom, we have supped at the table of freedom, and we should help to secure and to share the fruits of freedom for others. This is our manifest destiny!

The task of securing and maintaining freedom is a difficult one and a continuous one. It is also a frustrating task – long and involved, in which Korea was only the first frustration and Viet Nam not the last.

Because of our beliefs, because of our traditions and history, and because we have enjoyed the blessings of freedom, we must share our heritage with others. Because of our heritage we are committed to the struggle in Viet Nam, so others may have what we have already enjoyed.

I was surprised that this message gained wide acceptance, especially on the campus of Rutgers University where — I believe — young people desperately were seeking an understanding of America's involvement in Vietnam and the true meaning of "the domino effect."

Being asked to speak before other groups, I did and I didn't alter the message regardless of the setting. But, as I continued to carry the message, I began to realize two (2) things:

- That if the war continued for as long as I anticipated it would in the jungles of Asia, then my two (2) oldest boys would be involved since I had long ago imbued them with the concept of military service in defense of the nation's interests; and,
- That, essentially, I was asking young men to fight a war that "old men" said was just.

These realizations caused me to do two (2) things:

1. I began to require more of my sons in terms of responsibility and to encourage them to exert their own style of individual leadership. These two (2) characteristics, I believed, would stand in their favor if they ever needed to go into combat; and,
2. Believing that it was not right to ask others to do what I was not being asked to do, I volunteered for duty in Vietnam by writing to the Commandant of the United States Marine Corps and offering my services as a symbolic gesture to others. The reply to my offer to volunteer follows.

DEPARTMENT OF THE NAVY
HEADQUARTERS UNITED STATES MARINE CORPS
WASHINGTON, D.C. 20380

In Reply Refer To AQ-EWS-jth
21 Nov 1969

Mr. John B. Moullette
Lecturer in Education
Rutgers University
Department of Vocational-Technical Education
New Brunswick, New Jersey 08903

Dear Mr. Moullette:

Your letter of 17 November 1969 to the Commandant of the Marine Corps volunteering for 30 days duty in Vietnam has been referred to me for reply. It was received with interest and gratitude in the knowledge that patriotism still burns strong within individuals of this country.

An enlistment for a 30 day period of active duty with the U.S. Marine Corps in Vietnam, or elsewhere, is not authorized by existing regulations. The minimum length of enlistment is two years. As a former Marine, you can appreciate fully that this is a valid requirement.

Those of us who have been in Vietnam know fully, however, that America does not lack for true patriots within the ranks of the Armed Forces. The individual contributions of Marines and other servicemen to the eventual freedom of South Vietnam are almost legendary. But what we do lack is articulate, strong-willed Americans here at home who do not hesitate to express their appreciation of our efforts in South Vietnam and their support of our nation's objectives. We particularly feel this lack in the academic community.

I personally appreciate your generous offer to help, but I think your continued strong support on the campus – as evidenced by your papers – represents a source of encouragement we can ill afford to lose.

Sincerely,

D.T. Kane
Colonel, U.S. Marine Corps
Director, Policy Analysis Division

America's involvement in the Vietnam War ended – with the exception of the evacuation of Americans from Saigon in April 1975 – on 27 January 1973 with the signing of the Paris Peace Accord. Coincidentally, this was the same day that my oldest son – John – completed his Marine Corps boot camp training at Parris Island. Had the war lasted another six (6) months, his life would have experienced dramatic changes and – no doubt – so would mine and that of the entire Moullette family.

My mind has never changed — the war was a test of wills or, as General William C. Westmoreland, the American military commander in Vietnam — believed, it was a measure of our "resolve." In my opinion, the war was mismanaged from Washington and the wrong strategy was employed: the search and destroy strategy of seeking out the enemy in the jungle and Delta was foolish and smacked of the strategy planned for the Plains of Europe in the event the Communists pushed west from behind the Iron Curtain.

A more reasonable strategy would have been the one of consolidating positions in the urban areas of Saigon, Danang and Hue and working outward to "win the hearts and minds" of the Vietnamese.

The collapse of the Soviet Union in 1989 does not mean that the war in Vietnam was in vain. On the contrary, our resolve in Korea, Cuba, and Vietnam, our ability to finance a defense posture, our intellectual development of a technical and computer ability, and, our strong desire to spearhead freedom around the world contributed greatly to the humiliating defeat of communism and the Union of Soviet Socialist Republics.

The world owes a debt of gratitude to those who fought in Korea and Vietnam, and to those Americans who died in Asia -- more than 100,000 collectively for the two (2) campaigns.

As an aside to the comment regarding the Soviet Union: In the fall of 1984 I journeyed from London, England, to Kowloon, Hong Kong, by train. This trip took me across northern Europe, through Siberia, and south through Outer Mongolia and China.

During the passage, I crossed 10 of the 11 time zones that include the USSR, made extensive stopovers in the capital city of Moscow and the Lake Baikal city of Irkutsk, and minor layovers in nine (9) major cities across the USSR.

During that trip, I saw nothing that convinced me that the USSR was an industrial giant. Moscow was a dreary, drab city while Irkutsk was quaint but antiquated. Along the railroad route, Siberia reminded me of southern New Jersey of my boyhood days -- long stretches of dense pine forests and corduroy roads traveled by jalopies. For five (5) years after this trip -- until the fall of 1989 -- I remained baffled more by what I did not see rather than by what I did.

In the end, and with the fall of communism in the USSR, it turned out that Russia was an underdeveloped, third country nation with its citizens living on the edge of poverty and accepting the fate bestowed upon them by Lenin and Stalin. It was not an inheritance that would allow for national progress and individual initiative.

Concern for events in Southeast Asia continued – on my part – for many years to come. I continued to speak out for continued support of those to whom we had made promises and I continued to attempt to rally support in the American Congress. Eventually, the attempt faded away. Americans were tired of the events in Southwest Asia.

JOHN GLENN
OHIO
United States Senate
WASHINGTON. D.C. 20510
April 18, 1975

Mr. John B. Moullette
Department of Commerce
31 North Grant Avenue
Columbus, Ohio 43215

Dear Mr. Moullette:

I appreciated receiving your letter about President Ford's request for supplemental appropriations for South Viet Nam and Cambodia.

This has been a highly complex situation that has changed not only daily, but sometimes from hour to hour in recent weeks. The historical arguments concerning commitments and promises, and reasons for or against providing aid, appear to be overshadowed by events. I am sure we agree that as of now our only remaining problem is how to best extricate ourselves from the rapidly deteriorating situation with the least loss of lives.

The Cambodian situation is resolved, thankfully, with no loss of life, and with removal of all American personnel and close Cambodian supporters who might have been principal targets of reprisals as the Khmer Rouge forces move closer to complete takeover.

We must now accomplish the same thing in South Viet Nam, and that will not be easy with the larger numbers of people involved. There are thousands of Americans still in South Viet Nam and even much larger numbers of South Vietnamese who have worked closely enough with us to be targets for retribution if South Vietnam falls.

Within the next few days the Congress is expecting to receive information regarding the President's plan for accomplishing the withdrawal, and we must decide what, if any, additional authority the President needs. Last week, the President indicated in his Foreign Policy statement to the Congress that he tied much importance to additional appropriations for South Viet Nam, but additional funds are certainly not going to be the determining factor at this point.

Timing is of the utmost importance, and I hope the President is taking every action possible to get as many of our personnel out of Viet Nam now as he possibly can. I have repeatedly called for such action. To do otherwise is to make a bad situation ever more uncontrollable.

This is certainly not a time for political finger-pointing and blame-placing. There has already been too much of that, and with enough blame for many people through quite a number of Administrations.

28

But just looking back does little good. As the present tragedy passes we must make certain we never permit ourselves to again be drifted into ill-considered foreign commitments via the Executive Agreement route. I have introduced legislation to that effect which is now being considered in Committee.

Presidential and Congressional decisions and timing in the few days ahead may well determine the fate of many thousands of Americans and Vietnamese. I pray we all make those decisions wisely.

Sincerely,

John Glenn
United States Senator

ROBERT TAFT, JR.
OHIO
United States Senate
WASHINGTON. D.C. 20510
May 6, 1975

Mr. John B. Moullette
Division of State Fire Marshal
Department of Commerce
31 North Grant Avenue
Columbus, Ohio 43215

Dear Mr. Moullette:

Thank you for your communication regarding the situation in South Vietnam, and the problems that situation has created.

It is my belief that we had a responsibility to agree to provide military aid to South Vietnam for as long as that country had any chance to stabilize the military situation, and for as long as the South Vietnamese desired to continue to resist the North Vietnamese invasion.

I believe that our long-term encouragement of the South Vietnamese to resist North Vietnamese aggression created a moral requirement that we supply South Vietnam with the means of resistance. That requirement was strengthened by the Paris Peace Accords, which provided that we could, and, would, replace South Vietnamese war material losses on a one-for-one basis.

I am sorry that we failed to meet that commitment. Our failure is already leading to major policy reassessments by many of our allies. I fear that it will lead to major destabilization in the international arena, and to significant gains for the Soviet Union.

Humanitarian aid to refugees is another matter, and I fully support doing everything in our power to ease the human suffering of the South Vietnamese. I voted for the provision of humanitarian aid, and I support our efforts to rescue those who may face imprisonment or death at the hands of the victorious North Vietnamese. I think the efforts of the American people, as individuals, to give a new life to South Vietnamese children orphaned by the war, is the one bright spot in what is otherwise a very bleak picture. The question of supporting international agencies depends in my view on the programs and the assurance of proper administration to prevent any support of the Communist regime that seems inevitable.

In sum, the war is over. I worked for the provision of adequate military aid to South Vietnam, in the period when such aid might have made the difference; unfortunately, the majority of my colleagues in Congress did not agree with me. I hope that the international repercussions for our failure to support our ally will not be as severe as I am led to fear they will be.

Sincerely,

Robert Taft, Jr.

7 INTO THE BREECH

The Six Day War of 1967 between Israel and the Arabs was followed by the Middle East War of 1973 between the same parties. America, of course – along with the Netherlands – supported the State of Israel. As a result, the Arab members of the Organization of Petroleum Exporting Countries (OPEC) embargoed oil shipments to the United States that further resulted in a 400 percent increase in Arab oil. What once cost $2 per barrel now cost nearly $40 and gasoline prices immediately rose from 19.9 cents a gallon, and, ultimately, to more than $1.00 per gallon. Oil had become a bargaining lever in diplomacy. The Arab States, and especially, Saudi Arabia, Kuwait, and the Arab Emirates, had become economically important to America and to the industrial world.

My immediate concern was to juggle my household budget to match rising costs in heating oil and gasoline for the family automobile. There was little concern for the problems in the Mid-East.

This, of course, changed with my involvement with the Royal Saudi Navy at Dammam between 1977 and 1979 and, ultimately, with my employment in 1980 through 1989 with ARAMCO in Dhahran and Ras Tanura, Saudi Arabia.

Much of my tenure in Arabia would be highlighted by the war between the Muslim Arabs of Iraq and the Muslim Persians of Iran; but, my tenure would, also, witness the following:

- The taking and holding of American hostages in Tehran in 1979 and their subsequent release in 1981.
- The Arab Shiite revolt in Qatif, Saudi Arabia, in 1979; and, the Persian Shiite revolt at Mecca during the same period.
- The signing of the peace treaty between Sadat's Egypt and the State

of Israel in 1979.

- The Shiite Muslim rebellion in Syria in 1982, wherein thousands were massacred.
- The 1982 Israeli invasion of Lebanon and the U.S. Marine arrival in Beirut.
- The terrorist attack on the American Embassy and the Marines' Compound in Lebanon in 1983 where hundreds of Marines were killed, and, which resulted in the departure of the American Marines in 1984.
- The withdrawal of Israel from most of Lebanon in 1985.
- The Intifada revolt against the Israeli occupation of the West Bank and the Gaza Strip in 1987.
- The Iraqi attack on the American Frigate *USS Stark* in the Arabian (Persian) Gulf and the shooting down of the Iranian Airbus over the Gulf of Hormuz by the Americans in July of 1988; and,
- The recognition of Israel's right to exist by the Palestine Liberation Organization's (PLO's) Yassar Arafat in December 1988.

Both the Iraqi attack on the *Stark* and the American attack on the Airbus were declared "mistakes" during the heat of battle in the so-called "tanker war." In both cases, these occurrences took place within 100 miles of my home in Saudi Arabia with the war between Iraq and Iran being within 200 miles. These were exciting times -- not thought to be too dangerous – wherein Americans in the Middle East would become acutely aware of the Arabs' as well as the Muslims' attitudes toward the Israeli occupation of Palestine.

During this period of time I would become involved in two (2) organizations that would have a great interest in the events of the Middle East. The first would be the Dhahran Memorial Division, China Post #1, of the American Legion, Department of New York. The second would be the American Businessmen's Association (the ABA). Both were and are headquartered in Dhahran, Saudi Arabia. For the former, I would serve as Commander on two (2) occasions (1986-1987 and 1988-1989) and for the latter, I would serve on a steering committee to develop strategies for influencing American lawmakers with respect to the need for American business in Arabia.

The American Legion group was made up of men, primarily, who had worked around the world on projects deemed important to American political and business interests. They were acutely aware of the ongoing warfare between the Soviet Union and the United States and many had earned the sobriquet "soldier of fortune." In Arabia, they gave themselves the euphemism "Chinese Cooking Class" in order to mislead any Arab

Counter Intelligence Department (CID) personnel who might be looking for clandestine groups and from the Muslim religious police who were constantly looking for male/female fraternization and "bootleg" or black market booze.

Both groups decided it was time to let America's leaders know where the 40,000 Americans working and living in the Gulf stood on the moral issue of the Palestinians who had lost a homeland and on the economic issue of selling military hardware to the Arabs, and, especially, to the Saudis.

The first occasion fell to me when the Dhahran Memorial Division met in Manama, Bahrain, 25 through 28 March 1987, in the Diplomat Hotel. Guests in attendance were the American Ambassador to Bahrain – the Honorable Dr. Samir H. Zakhem – and the Commander of the American Task Force in the Arabian (Persian) Gulf – Rear Admiral Harold J. Bernsen.

The full text of my speech follows.

Dhahran Memorial Division
China Post #1
American Legion
Department of New York

Mr. Ambassador and Admiral H.J. Bernsen – the Dhahran Memorial Division of China Post #1, American Legion, Department of New York, welcomes you and your ladies to its annual celebration of the Chinese New Year.

China Post #1 – facetiously but with cautious reason – is often referred to as the Chinese Cooking Class in Dhahran. This is a unique post of the American Legion. Its 'flag' has never been home to the United States and its founding documents are lost 'somewhere' on mainland China. The Post was founded there in 1920. It has operated in exile – the only American Legion Post to do so – since 1948, when the Communist influence and eventually the Communist 'hold' forced us out of China. We hope to return.

Mr. Ambassador and Admiral Bernsen, the 57 Americans here this evening represent the finest that America has to offer in the way of professional, managerial, engineering and technical skills. Here -- in the Gulf -- they are the epitome of American greatness. There are men and women in this gathering who – here in the Middle East:

- have drilled the deepest oil wells in the world.
- have lifted the highest volume of oil – on a daily basis – from the bowels of the earth.
- have engineered the most sophisticated pipeline, communications, and highway systems.

- have provided the highest quality medical services.
- have managed the construction of schools and cities; and, generally
- have contributed to the development and expansion of a desert nation so that it can be brought abreast of the 20th Century and prepared for the 21st.

The Dhahran Memorial Division is, indeed, a unique group of Americans. The men in attendance this evening – as well as some of the women – have served their Country and the principles for which it stands during:

- World War II
- the Berlin Blockade
- the Korean Conflict
- the continuous 'cold war'; and, more recently
- the terrible conflict in Southeast Asia.

One of the Post's members -- not here this evening -- was a recent Nicaraguan 'prisoner of war.'

These people subscribe to Gunnery Sergeant Highway's observation that since 1940 we Americans have:

- won one
- tied one
- lost one

And, they ask the same question as Rambo: "Next time, will we be allowed to win?'

Because, Mr. Ambassador and Admiral Bernsen, this group of Americans is – really – not accustomed to losing. We subscribe to Vince Lombardi's point of view: 'Winning isn't everything, but losing is nothing!'

We hope, Mr. Ambassador, that you will report to those people whom you represent that the Americans in this part of the world are not entirely happy with American foreign policy, especially as it is practiced in the Middle East. A more evenhanded approach is called for.

And, Admiral Bernsen, we trust you will recognize that the same American spirit that helped free the conquered nations of Western Europe, that raised the American flag over countless islands in the Pacific and faced down the 'Communist armed threat' throughout the world is still alive.

And, we hope you both will understand that because of the investments we and our comrades have made in the preservation and the extension of freedom that we do not want our sons and our grandsons – and perhaps our daughters and granddaughters – to be exploited in world situations that have not been carefully thought through and skillfully planned and executed.

We are the kind of people, gentlemen, who can move any mountain if we are sufficiently motivated and truthfully led.

This, then, Mr. Ambassador and Admiral Bernsen, is the American Legion in the Middle East.

Welcome! We look forward to our visit with you, an interesting evening, and to your points of view relative to this geo-political area.

The message here – obliquely put – was that:

1. The Americans – since 1933 – had a vested interest in the Middle East.
2. The Americans working and living in the Middle East were not strangers to danger.
3. The Americans, especially those with military backgrounds, never again wanted to be placed in a non-winning situation when it comes to American military involvement.
4. The Americans – watching events in the Middle East from their strategic and unique viewpoint – were not happy with the Executive Branch's, as well as the Legislative Branch's, bias in favor of the State of Israel.
5. The Americans in the Gulf would be sending this message – in various forms – home.

With respect to Point 5, we knew that both the Ambassador and the Admiral were duty-bound to report back to their superiors the trends that were developing in the American communities in the Middle East.

Salaamu Alaykum

Once again it is my pleasure to welcome the members of the Dhahran Memorial Division, China Post #1, American Legion, Department of New York, and our ladies to the Division's annual convention in the State of Bahrain.

And, again, it is a high honor to welcome Dr. Sam Zakhem, the American Ambassador to the State of Bahrain and Admiral Anthony

Less, the Commander of the Middle East Task Force. Additionally, it is a pleasure to have the former American Ambassador to Djibouti with us. Gentlemen, it is a pleasure to have you and Mrs. Less with us this evening. And, we look forward to your comments relative to this geo-political area.

I believe you will agree that it is always inspirational to watch any color guard of the United States Marine Corps post the National colors and the Marine Corps standard. For this – this evening – we are indebted to Gunnery Sergeant Carl J. Fuselier of the Marine Security Guard, of the American Embassy, in the State of Bahrain. Marines, thank you. And, we welcome you and your ladies to our annual event. Semper fi!

Before we continue, permit me to introduce the Division members to our guests – Ambassador, Doctor Zakhem, Ambassador Ferriter, and Admiral Less. Gentlemen, and Mrs. Less, the men and women this evening are America's ambassadors to the Kingdom of Saudi Arabia. All of the men, and a few of the women, are wartime veterans – spanning the period from World War II through Vietnam.

And, each person in attendance is making a contribution to the development of the Kingdom of Saudi Arabia. This is an effort to bring the Kingdom abreast of the 20th Century and prepared for the 21st. No easy task, this; but, it is one that the men and women in attendance are well prepared. They have been steeped in the tradition of: 'doing the difficult immediately while doing the impossible takes just a little longer.'

Last year, Mr. Ambassador, this group of Americans asked you to carry a message to those you represent. And, that message was and still is: 'American foreign policy as it is practiced in the Middle East needs to be more evenhanded.' We believe you carried that message as we bear witness to the Schultz initiative currently taking place in the troublesome eastern Mediterranean. Thank you, Mr. Ambassador.

But, now, we have a second message and that is 'Americans want no part of a heavy hand where the victims have no say in the kind of lives they want to live, where they want to live.' It is absurd that the victims of a holocaust are now the perpetrators of inhuman acts. Americans, Mr. Ambassador, of all nationalities, will not stand for that – for long!

Last year, too, we asked the Commander of the Middle East Task Force and the people he represents not to exploit American lives "in world situations that have not been carefully thought through and skillfully planned and executed.' Fortunately, Admiral Less, there is no 'stark' evidence that this request has not been honored. And, we – as well as the back-home American public – are indebted to you, your predecessor, and the members of your command. Please express our thanks to them, for a job well done, in the finest traditions of the American military.

The members of your command are always welcome in our homes in the Eastern Province of Saudi Arabia when their ships dock in Dammam or Jubail. We promise to return them 'on time' – clean and sober.

This, then, Ambassador Zakhem, Ambassador Ferriter, guest Jack McCrain*, and Admiral and Mrs. Less, is the American Legion in the Middle East.

It is good to be here; and, it is good to see each and every one of you here this evening. Now, let us break bread together."

The Executive Committee of the Dhahran Memorial Division, American Legion, believed that – since the audience was changing – it was not necessary to alter the message. And, in 1989, the task – again – fell to me during my second stint as Commander. Dr. Samir H. Zakhem was still Ambassador to Bahrain whereas the Commander of the Mideast Task Force had changed. Both would remain in their positions through the 1990-1991 Gulf War (Desert Shield and Desert Storm). One would go home with honors and immediate retirement from the U.S. Navy, and the other to retirement from Government Service.

---

* President of the Vinnell Corporation, providing training for the Saudi Arabian National Guard.

Remarks of
John B. Moullette, Ed.D.
Commander
Dhahran Memorial Division
1988-1989
Regency Hotel
Bahrain

Salaamu Alaykum!! Welcome to Bahrain.

Our reasons for being here this evening are: to celebrate Chinese New Year, belatedly; to welcome Rear Admiral William M. Fogarty, Commander of the Mideast Task Force, and his wife Dawn, to this part of the world; and, to pay honor and tribute to the American Ambassador to the State of Bahrain – Dr. Samir H. Zakhem and his wife Marilyn, who is currently out of the country.

In welcoming Admiral and Mrs. Fogarty to this part of the world, and to our Convention, we would like them to know something about the men and women here this evening.

First of all, our membership of 150 veterans – of three (3) major 20th Century conflicts – support you and your command for the Command's efforts and presence in the Arabian Gulf. And, we show our support by our active involvement in the 'take a sailor to dinner' program when the ships of the fleet dock in Dammam and – when possible – in Jubail. And, in critical situations – such as the 3 July 1988 event in the Gulf – we are quick to inform the Commander-in-Chief, Admiral, of our support of those who must make command decisions in the heat of battle. Your predecessors – Admirals Bernsen and Less – have had our support when they needed it most. Please be assured, Admiral, you will have that support, also.

Secondly, Admiral and Mrs. Fogarty, the men and women here this evening are the epitome of American greatness.

These, Admiral and Mrs. Fogarty, are your countrymen in the Middle East, and – just as importantly – your comrades in arms. We are happy that you have joined us this evening.

This is an evening of pleasure and we won't stand on ceremony before the pleasure starts; but, I have been charged by my colleagues to leave the Ambassador and the Admiral with the following messages. The Dhahran Memorial Division, China Post #1, American Legion, would like you both to make the following points to those people you represent in Washington, D.C.

Gentlemen:

America needs to apply an even hand in the Eastern Mediterranean toward the Palestinians in accordance with UN Resolutions 181, 242 and 338; and, in accordance with America's concept of 'free choice.'

America needs to extend a compassionate view and a helping hand to those Arabs in the West Bank and Gaza Strip; and, to announce a firm rejection of Israeli, oppressive measures; this, in accordance with the Helsinki Agreements of 1975 and America's belief in common decency.

America needs to illustrate the military/political recognition that the moderate Arab States require local, defense deterrence, support and to have America's assurance of their legitimate security and defense requirements; this, in accordance with America's need for Arab oil, strategic support, and moderate Arab friends.

America needs to initiate efforts to capture a larger share of the Gulf States' import market simply by American industry getting in harmony with product standards of the five (5) Gulf Cooperative Council (GCC) States; this, in order to decrease America's trade imbalance and increase employment at home.

Every billion dollar increment in additional U.S. exports creates 25,000 to 30,000 jobs in the United States.

To summarize: We Americans in the Mideast believe in 'fair play' as a principle of American democracy and we strongly object to losing jobs and trade dollars because of Congressional naiveté' or submission to biased lobby groups – whether it be the loss of pipeline sales to the Soviet Union or the loss of military sales to Saudi Arabia.

If technology is going to be sold around the world, it might just as well be American technology; and, if military aircraft are to fly over the Gulf States for defensive and protective purposes, those planes ought be marked: 'Made in America.'

Again, Mr. Ambassador and Rear Admiral Fogarty and Mrs. Fogarty – welcome to our Convention. Thank you for joining us and thank you for breaking bread with us. We look forward to some 'words' from the Ambassador and from the Admiral on what can be expected in the Mideast now that the Bush Administration is in place and the Iran/Iraq Conflict has a 'cease fire.'

The obvious change in the message was occasioned by the American loss of a major aircraft contract to the British. (Time, 25 July 1988). Again, the Executive Committee of the Dhahran Memorial Division saw this as an uninformed bias against Saudi Arabia and a direct response to politics by the American Congress. And, the ABA saw this as a threat to American interests in the Gulf. Both organizations decided to initiate a personal, as well as an organizational, effort to right the imbalance. The ABA initiated in

1988 a Washington Doorknock program wherein Americans from the Association going home on leave would stop off in Washington and "meet" with their representatives to get the message across. Those who stayed behind would become letter-writers. Mine started in July 1988 and concluded in July 1992.

In the spring of 1989,1 decided to end my career with ARAMCO. Prior to leaving in July of 1989, I was asked by the Executive Committee of the ABA to leave some thoughts behind; those thoughts follow.

American Businessmen's Association
(ABA)
Luncheon Meeting
20 June 1989
Meridien Hotel — Dhahran

The position of the American Businessmen's Association (ABA) in Saudi Arabia with respect to defense and security is that

1. Moderate Arab member states of the Gulf Cooperation Council (GCC) require an adequate, local defense deterrence.
2. Arabian Gulf stability is vital to American interests.
3. America needs:
    *   Arab oil.
    *   Arab political support.
    *   Arab strategic support.
4. America owes it to the moderate Arab states to assure their legitimate security and defense requirements.
5. Congress' denial of legitimate GCC defense requests:
    *   Strains America's relationships with the moderate Arab states.
    *   Causes the moderate Arab states to seek assistance elsewhere.
    *   Lessens America's influence in the Middle East.

Foreign military sales generate American jobs, personal income, corporate profits, and tax revenues.

American support of the moderate Arab states is essential to American diplomatic, strategic and economic interests.

It was a short but succinct message and would prove viable by 02 August 1990 when the Iraqi Arabs would attempt to annex Kuwait, which would result in the Gulf War.

8 WINDING DOWN

02 August 1990 found me visiting friends in Maine with whom I had worked and socialized while in Saudi Arabia. A few days earlier, I had completed a wilderness survival program of 10 days in Vermont and I was working my way east and north to Quebec by automobile.

While shaving – prior to departure that day – a knock came on the bathroom door accompanied by my friend's shouted questions: "Guess what that crazy son-of-a-bitch has done?" Having been isolated for nearly two (2) weeks, I wasn't aware of recent domestic situations let alone international. So, I asked: "Who?" And, he answered: "Hussein!" "King Hussein (of Jordan)?" I asked. "No, Saddam Hussein of Iraq. His forces have invaded Kuwait!"

And, that is how I learned that the balance of power on the Arabian Peninsula had been tilted. Saudi Arabia's perceived threat from Iran across the Gulf was shelved, at least temporarily, since it was inconceivable that Iraq and Iran would join forces to march down the eastern side of the peninsula and occupy all the oil fields from Kuwait to Oman via Bahrain, Qatar and the Emirates.

Discussing the situation over coffee, my friend and I concluded that this unprovoked act on Saddam Hussein's part was simply an act to gain more oil to feed his military complex and to gain access to the Gulf for shipping purposes since the Shart al-Arab at the confluence of the Tigris and Euphrates Rivers was still in dispute between Iraq and Iran. The recent 10-year war between the two (2) nations did not settle that argument and Iran was still in possession of the deep water port at Abadan. It was further concluded that the oil fields of Saudi Arabia and its deep water ports of al-Jubail, Ras Tanura, and Dammam were in serious danger. Concluding that, I bid my friend "good-bye" and proceeded on my way to Quebec and Montreal, Canada.

As I drove, I became confident – that even though my friends in Saudi Arabia were in jeopardy – there were several scenarios with respect to military assistance that would protect them. Those scenarios were:

1. The American, forward area, military forces – based on the Indian Ocean island of Diego Garcia in the Chagos Archipelago – would be deployed immediately to protect the oil fields and ports in the Eastern Province of Saudi Arabia as would be the rapid deployment forces out of the United States and Western Europe; and,

2. Should American Forces not be readily available, then elements of the Israeli Army would "hard charge" down the American built TAPLINE Road that joined the Mediterranean with the Gulf and set-up defensive positions or engage in defensive activities until the Americans arrived to protect those oil fields in eastern Arabia. Those oil fields were/are not only vital to America's industrial empire but, also, are vital to the rest of the world's.

Now, the latter scenario was/is fraught with all kinds of problems as far as the Middle East is concerned; and, – I'm satisfied – that scenario would have been employed had not scenario number one (1) worked.

Upon my arrival in Quebec, I took a quick look around and continued on to Montreal and recrossed the border into the United States. There, I "holed up" for one (1) short night. In the morning, I made a straight-through drive to my home in Florida. On arrival, the phone was "ringing off the hook" with calls of American friends in Saudi Arabia seeking information about America's intentions as reported in the news media. And, based on CNN's coverage of American military departures I could predict when those forces would land in Dhahran, Saudi Arabia. That consoled many of my friends and their families. But, two (2) families requested and received permission to use my home on a temporary basis.

Early in September, I received a call from a Commodore in the Royal Saudi Naval Forces (RSNF) requesting that I come to Saudi Arabia and take over an element of naval training while he returned to a combat position. This, I agreed to and I departed for Saudi Arabia in October.

Arriving in Saudi Arabia, I found the Saudis, and especially the Shiites, concerned and worried, while the expatriates were relatively calm and going about the business of operating enterprises, and, especially the oil industry, in a very professional manner. The same was not true for the RSNF at Dammam and I spent the next four (4) months observing the allied military build-up, attempting to revitalize a demoralized Saudi Naval training command, watching the engagements between SCUDS and PATRIOTS, and attempting to assure my daughters – by telephone – that I was safe.

Returning to the United States in the Spring of 1991, 1 was asked to share my experiences with the members of the Greater Clearwater (Florida) Council - 381, Navy League of the United States (NLUS) of which I am a Charter Member. This, I did and I entitled my presentation: 'Perspectives of a Persian Gulf Navy on the Contemporary Scene." I shared this presentation with two (2) former American Naval Task Force Commanders in the Middle East whom I had met while they were managing American Navy activities in the Persian Gulf during the "tanker war" in – what the Saudis like to call – the Arabian Gulf. Their responses follow.

**Perspectives of a
Persian Gulf Navy
and
Implications for
America's Maritime Strategy**

The Persian Gulf Navy I have in mind is the Saudi Navy, generally referred to as the Royal Saudi Naval Forces, or the RSNF.

From 1977 through 1979, I served as counterpart Manager for Education and Training for the Dammam Naval Training Center – today referred to as the Technical Institute of Naval Studies, or TINS.

In the summer of 1990 – during Operation Desert Shield – and, at the invitation of the TINS' Base Commander (a Saudi Commodore), I returned, on a consulting basis, to pursue three (3) objectives:

1. To evaluate the current basic sailor training program
2. To recommend program integration between the Saudi Navy's basic sailor training program, and basic technical, or "A" school training; and,
3. To formulate a structure of a Saudi Navy Central Training Command, or CENTRACOM.

This assignment called for:

- Identifying strengths and weaknesses in the basic sailor training program.
- Pinpointing overlap and duplicity in basic sailor training and basic "A" school training; and,
- Recommending a command structure and organization for:

  o   the coordination of training within Naval Forces Schools;
  o   the budgeting of training monies;

o   the development of training curriculum;

o   the preparation of naval instructors;

o   procedures for operation and maintenance of training facilities; and,

o   training quality assurance.

(TWO [2] STAR FLAG)
DEPUTY CHIEF OF NAVAL OPERATIONS
(PLANS, POLICY AND OPERATIONS)
WASHINGTON, DC 20350
26 March 1991

Dear Dr. Moullette,

Thank you for sending me a copy of your presentation, "Perspectives of a Persian Gulf Navy on the Contemporary Scene." My strategy and policy staffs and I have read the speech with particular interest. We all found it to be an insightful and enlightening profile of the Saudi people, culture and naval forces.

As you can imagine, the Navy leadership is presently hard at work determining our future involvement in the Persian Gulf Theater, and relationships with the nations and navies of the area. Your perspective is indeed useful in this effort.

I applaud your involvement in the Navy League, and share your concerns regarding the Merchant Marine and Ready Reserve Fleet. Secretary of the Navy Garrett, in his recent Posture Statement, cited Navy involvement in the Congressional Mobility Requirements Study to determine our sealift requirements and options. In the meantime, the Navy budget contains $1.2 billion over the FY92-97 period for procurement of sealift ships. The Administration, Congress and the American people must decide the fate of our Merchant Marine; the Navy League plays an important role in fostering this cause.

Again, I thank you for your presentation, and active interest in the Nation's maritime strength. To support this continued interest, I have provided the attached brochure regarding aircraft carrier battle groups. Best wishes to you and your son -- my former Shipmate.

Sincerely,
A.A. LESS
Rear Admiral, U.S. Navy

(TWO [2] STAR FLAG)
DIRECTOR FOR PLANS AND POLICY
COMMANDER IN CHIEF UNITED STATES ATLANTIC FLEET
NORFOLK, VIRGINIA 23511-6001

08 April 1991

Dear John,

Thanks for sending me a copy of your presentation. It was very interesting and I enjoyed reading the paper, in particular your assessment of the Saudi character and work ethic. It is indeed a challenge for them to form any "real" military force.
A lot has happened since we met in Bahrain in 1987. I suspect the Island has undergone changes from which it may never recover. It would be interesting to pay a visit to see first hand.
Good hearing from you. Keep up the good work

Sincerely,

HJ. Bernsen
Rear Admiral, U.S. Navy

[The full text of "Perspective of a Persian Gulf Navy" may be found in the archives of the Proceedings magazine of the U.S. Naval Institute.]

Being a member of the Propeller Club of the United States, Port-of-Tampa, Florida, I was asked to share my experiences with the membership, which I agreed to do.

Since the Propeller Club's major tenet is "To promote, further and support an American Merchant Marine," I decided to expand the original speech by adding a few concepts relative to the situation facing the American Merchant Marine and a few social situations facing America's seapower forces. I retitled the speech and presented it at the 10 September 1991 meeting at the Tampa Yacht Club.

9 BOWING OUT – ALMOST

At this writing and with respect to world affairs, two (2) invitations are in – neither of which has been firmed up. The two (2) are:

- An International Labour Office (ILO) invitation to serve as an "Expert in Monitoring and Evaluation (sic) of Vocational Training Activities" in Islamabad, Pakistan; and,
- An invitation from the United Nations to provide "Employment and Training Needs Assessment" in Phnom Pen, Kampuchea (Cambodia).

The latter was chosen. [Please see Bibliography.]

Both assignments promise extensive travel in the host countries and both require extensive interaction with in-country nationals. Both are conducive to my interests with respect to foreign travel and interesting assignments.

However, both are fraught with the potential for personal danger. There is ongoing dissension on the sub-continent of India between the Indians and the Pakistanis; religious fundamentalism is rampant in both countries. And, the Khmer Rouge is still an active organization in Cambodia. Americans – especially those with white faces – are often the targets for those experiencing the frustrations in life faced by those who have not been blessed with a truly democratic birthright.

But, one must do what one must do; and if my end must come in either of the two (2) places, I trust it will be quick and not messy.

Spreading the fruits of an educated, industrial-technical society to those who are striving to raise themselves from the boundaries of poverty and illiteracy is worth the try and the gamble. I don't profess to be an Albert

Schweitzer, but I have no objection to following in his footprints.

American Involvements
in
Post Cold War
Military Actions

With the demise of the Soviet Union in 1987 and the ending of the so called Cold War, the people of the world saw the threat of annihilation removed from their daily lives and were hopeful they might get back to a way of life as experienced prior to World War II. What they didn't realize was that the stand-off between the two super powers was the glue that held the world together and lessened internecine differences among nations.

Immediately after the 'stand down', the people of the world realized old animosities – some ancient; some recent – were surfacing again and which centered on differences in culture and in religion.

The differences between Israel and Pakistan was one, Iran and Iraq another and Kosovo yet another. America's involvement in the mid-east and, especially, in the Persian Gulf area was paramount to the defense of allies and to the continuance of an essential supply line of oil for industrial nations in all hemispheres.

The occurrences started, initially – with the Tanker War (1987-1989), the Iraqi invasion of Kuwait with the follow up of Desert Shield and Desert Storm (1991). These were followed by the Al Qaeda bombings of American Embassies in Africa (1998) and the Al Qaeda attacks on America in New York City, the Pentagon and Shanksville, PA, known the world over as 9-11 (2001).

These were followed by the American incursion in Afghanistan (2001) and continued with the attack and war on Iraq (2003-2011). The engagement in Afghanistan continues at this writing and promises an ending in 2014. If the promise holds it would round out a century of war for Americans (1914-2014).

10 AFTERWORD

That young American Marine who, in 1919, stood among fallen Marines in the Marine Corps cemetery in Belleau Wood, France and who had a fetish for poetry asked: "After Armistice," 'How many more must die, O God? How many more must lie beneath the sod...?' got his answer – posthumously – 95 years later with "A Soldier's Reverie," 'Crosses, crosses, always crosses...'*

Alas, too many, too many, far too many!

Anon?

*Collected Poetry of Clarence Earle Moullette, 1897-1972, an anthology, 2013, pages 4 and 5.

BIBLIOGRAPHY

Brewer, Susan. *Why America Fights*. 2009, Oxford University Press.

Bundy, McGeorge, editor with Dean Acheson. *The Pattern of Responsibility*. 1952, Houghton Mifflin

Casey, Steven. *Selling the Korean War*. 2008, Oxford University Press.

Fischer, John. *Master Plan USA*. 1951, Harper & Brothers.

Jager, Sheila Miyoshi. *Brothers At War*. 2013, W.W. Norton & Company, Inc.

Moullette, John B., editor. *Collected Poetry of Clarence Earle Moullette*, 1897-1972, an anthology, 2013, CreateSpace, ISBN 978-1494242633

Moullette, John B. *International Relations*, Selected Speeches…. 1993, private printing, copyrighted.

Moullette, John B., Ed.D. *Experiences in Cambodia with the International Labor Organization* …., 1993-1994, private printing, copyrighted.

Moullette, John B. *Down to the Sea Again*. 2013, CreateSpace, ISBN 978-1484944257, copyrighted.

COMMENDATIONS AND AWARDS

United States Marine Corps
Honorable Discharge
as Testimonial of Fidelity and Obedience
25 August 1946

Temple University High School
Diploma for Completion of Studies prescribed for the Academic Course
05 September 1950

United States Marine Corps
Honorable Discharge
as a Testimonial of Honest and Faithful Service
15 May 1952

New Jersey State College
Degree of Bachelor of Science in Education
15 June 1957

Rutgers University
Honorary Societies

Epsilon Pi Tau
Fall 1966
Phi Delta Kappa
Winter 1967

Rutgers University
Degree of Master of Education
25 January 1966

Rutgers University
Degree of Doctor of Education
03 June 1970

The Flag of the United States of America
flown over The United States Capitol
in Honor of John B. Moullette
17 February 1984

American Legion
Dhahran, Saudi Arabia
In Appreciation for Serving as Commander
1986 and 1987
and
Outstanding Service to the
Dhahran Memorial Division
China Post #1

Marine Resources Development Foundation
Presentation of the Aquanaut Certificate
For Living and Working in the
Marine Resources Underwater Laboratory
for Twenty-four Hours or More
April 1990

Rutgers University
and the
Graduate School of Education
Presentation of the
Distinguished Service Award
To John B. Moullette
M.Ed. '66 & Ed.D. '70
In Recognition of
Outstanding Contributions to Education
07 March 1992

The Marquis Publications Board Certifies that
John Brinkley Moullette
is a subject of biographic records in the 56th edition of
Who's Who in America
2002

ABOUT THE AUTHOR

John B. Moullette has traveled extensively throughout the world and has worked at sea as well as on land with the peoples of many different nations. He makes his home in Fort Garland, Colorado.